Thomas Becket
of Canterbury

Patron of the Church in England
and the English Pastoral Clergy

by
J. B. Midgley

*All booklets are published thanks to the
generous support of the members of the
Catholic Truth Society*

CATHOLIC TRUTH SOCIETY
PUBLISHERS TO THE HOLY SEE

Contents

Politics and Religion

Some years ago when the media were inviting opinions on the great Englishmen of history, some nominated Thomas Becket only for others to dismiss him as one whose dangerous views could cause civil unrest. Their view was that he had defended the cause of Christianity and the law of the Church to the disadvantage of the State, and placed obedience to God above that owed to a temporal ruler. They missed the point that there is no conflict of interest since in pursuing the benefit of society the activities of both Church and State are interdependent. It is sensible to remember, however, that the relationship between religion and politics, God and Mammon, Church and State, remains subject to potential tension until the end of time when God the Son returns in glory to present a perfect Kingdom to His Father. Thomas died for the general principle of the Church's freedom and "Our crime", he wrote, "is the assertion of ecclesiastical liberty; for to profess it is, according to our prosecutor, to be guilty of high treason."

As Patron of the English Pastoral Clergy, he gives eager support to prayers that generous souls will answer God's call to the ministerial priesthood in the one, holy,

Catholic, and apostolic Church. He says, "Many are needed to plant the word, and many to water it. The spread of the faith and the increase in population demand this. God's people of old who had only one altar, still needed many teachers. How much greater now are the needs of this gathering of nations, for whose sacrifices Lebanon itself could not provide enough firewood; nor could all Judea provide enough animals for victims." He speaks to the Shepherds of the Flock about their responsibility in the Church to guard the teaching of the Apostles under the authority of the Pope who is the Bishop of Rome.

"If we care about what we are said to be, if we want to realise fully what it means that people call us bishops and high priests, then we ought to contemplate continuously and deeply the example of Him whom God made High Priest for ever, and walk in His ways. We have been appointed his representatives on earth; we have succeeded the Apostles as heads of the churches. By our ministry, the kingdom of death and sin is to be destroyed and Christ's building is to grow into a holy temple in the Lord, held together by faith and increasing holiness.

"Who can doubt that the Church of Rome is the head of all the churches and the source of Catholic teaching? Who does not know that the keys of the Kingdom of Heaven were given to Peter? Is not the whole structure and tradition of the Church built on Peter's faith, so to grow until we all meet Christ as one perfect Man, united in faith and in our recognition of him as the Son of God?

"It is Peter to whom major judgements concerning God's people are entrusted when they are submitted to the Bishop of Rome. Under him, the other officers of Mother Church are organised in so far as they are called to share in his responsibility and exercise the power entrusted to them" (cf. *Office of Readings*, Feast of St Thomas).

Downham Market, December 29th, 2007

Early Life

Gilbert Becket was born in Rouen and his wife Matilda in Caen. Like many Normans, they had come to England to make their fortune, and Gilbert's eventual royal appointment as Sheriff of London indicated their success and affluence. On 21st December 1118, at the family home in Poultry, Matilda gave birth to a son who, within a matter of hours, was taken to St Mary Colchurch where he was baptized and christened Thomas after the Apostle whose feast, prior to 1970, coincided with his birthday. William FitzStephen, later a close friend and biographer of Thomas, tells us that Matilda dreamt she had been carrying the whole church of Canterbury in her womb, and that when the nurse first received the new born babe she announced, "I have raised from the ground a future Archbishop." History does not mention any other children, so this son was especially dear to his parents.

Education

By the beginning of the twelfth century, the Anglo-Saxons had come to terms with the inevitable, and overcome their Norman conquerors by absorbing them. The resultant "English" population was characterised by

King Henry I who was born and educated in England, and whose reign brought the atmosphere of comparative calm in which Thomas enjoyed his boyhood. His education began at the Augustinian Priory in Merton and continued at St Paul's Cathedral School only a sort walk from the Becket home. The young scholar showed a natural aptitude in his studies and impressed his teachers though, at this stage, he was not an avid pursuer of learning. At the same time, Gilbert arranged he should learn the social accomplishments of a gentleman that included swordsmanship, falconry, hunting, dancing, and the savoir-faire of a courtier under the tuition of his friend Richer de l'Aigle. Probably at some stage Thomas also received the tonsure, for it was common for privileged young men to receive this first order of clerical status so that they were eligible to receive or inherit an ecclesiastical benefice, or as a convenient starting point in the event of a later decision to pursue a career in the Church without an obligation to do so.

When he was fifteen, Thomas was admitted to the University of Paris, then enjoying a reputation as a place of learning where eminent teachers of the day included Peter Abelard and Peter Lombard. He was to spend the next seven years here, and the studies he undertook and his contact with fine minds helped fashion his character and foster his attitudes and values. One of his fellow students was John of Salisbury who, one day, would become secretary to Archbishop Theobald of Canterbury, Bishop of Chartres, and a lifelong friend and biographer.

Fortunes change

Now twenty-two, Thomas finally returned home in 1140, but it was to an England much changed from the one he had known. Because Henry I's heir Prince William had drowned in the White Ship tragedy of 1120, the King had arranged that his daughter Matilda, wife of Geoffrey of Anjou, should succeed him. However, when he died in 1135, many English nobles were reluctant to accept the rule of a Queen, and this antipathy gave Stephen, William the Conqueror's grandson, the opportunity to seize the throne. Not to be deterred, Matilda came from Normandy to claim her crown and won the support of the West of England, but the East sided with Stephen. The inevitable disturbance and confusion in the land had an impact on the Becket fortunes that had already suffered as a result of the fire that devastated London in 1136. Thomas began work at once to help repair the family's losses as a notary in Richer de l'Aigle's offices and in the country house of another family friend, Osbert Huitderniers who was Justiciar of London, experience that was to stand him in good stead.

Employed at Canterbury

Gilbert and Matilda Becket both died within a few months of each other, and in 1142 another family friend,

Archdeacon Baldwin, who would later become Bishop of Worcester and Archbishop of Canterbury (1185 - 1190), introduced Thomas to Archbishop Theobald of Canterbury who was so impressed that he instantly appointed him to a position in his household and curial offices. There he found himself in the scintillating company of gifted men whom the Archbishop gathered around him, but one was jealous of the favour shown to the newcomer. Roger de Port l'Eveque, who was destined to become Archbishop of York, made life difficult for him and remained an enemy for the rest of his life.

Thomas was not yet able to match his colleagues in learning and experience, but he outshone them in character. He was also blessed with a head for detail and a flair for getting things done efficiently with tact and charm. When Pope Innocent II died in 1143, Archbishop Theobald wanted to see his successor Celestine II as soon as possible. He hoped he would be able to persuade the new Pope to transfer the office of Papal Legate to Canterbury from Winchester, and seek approval and support for the House of Anjou's claim to the English throne. He chose Thomas to accompany him to Rome, and that the mission was successful in each case was due to the sound sense and skill with which the young man presented the arguments. As a result, the Plantagenet descendants of Geoffrey of Anjou were to provide England with rulers from Henry II to Richard II.

In 1145, Theobald sent Thomas to Bologna to study under the great Benedictine teacher John Gratian who had just completed his *Concordance of Disordant Canons*, or the *Decretum Gratiani*. This work effectively introduced the idea of the Church being centrally governed from Rome, and curtailed royal and secular interference in ecclesiastical affairs. This massive compilation of four thousand canonical rulings, organised in a hundred 'distinctions' and thirty-six 'cases', became the standard Canon Law textbook until the Church's legal reform in 1917. Celestine II's papacy lasted only seven months and that of his successor Lucius II less than a year, but the election in 1145 of the holy Cistercian Blessed Eugenius III heralded a reign of eight years. In 1147, Matilda of Anjou decided her position was untenable and returned to Normandy. The competition with Stephen that had divided the country with unhappy consequences prompted Theobald to go to Eugenius hoping to enlist his support for Henry Platagenet's succession to the English throne, and with him went Thomas and Roger de Port l'Eveque. In debate with Roger who supported the claims of Stephen, Thomas successfully promoted the cause of the son of Geoffrey and Matilda of Anjou.

Wealth and honour

Passing reference has already been made to the mediaeval practice of using the income and benefices attached to ecclesiastical positions for the benefit of clergy. This was especially so in the case of clerics employed in the chancelleries of bishops and royal households who paid substitute vicars a small stipend to undertake their responsibility for the care of souls, and it was not long before wealth and honour came Thomas' way. He was given the livings of St Mary le Strand in London, Otford in Kent, appointed prebendary canon of St Paul's and Lincoln and, as soon as he was ordained deacon, provost of Beverley. By happy chance, the scholarly John of Salisbury, the friend from Paris days, had now entered the service of Archbishop Theobald thanks to an introduction from by St Bernard of Clairvaux.

John could skilfully relate theory to practice, particularly when addressing the burning question of the time about the precise relationship between Church and State in matters of government. In his great work, *The Policraticus* that he dedicated to Thomas, he gives an exposition of a theocracy, a State where God rules, and explains that while Church and State play their part in the life of Christendom, the State is only the body while the Church is the soul on which the unity of the whole depends. In such a union, a king is God's minister in temporal matters and is therefore a semi-ecclesiastical official, a "*persona mixta*" but, precisely because of his concern with material affairs, his laws and authority must be subordinate to those of the Church. With all of this

Thomas agreed as it was very much in accord with what Gratian had taught him in Bologna.

By the time he was thirty-five, Thomas Becket's training and preparation were at their peak. William FitzStephen says "he was handsome and pleasing of countenance, tall of stature, with a prominent and aquiline nose, nimble and active in his movements, gifted with eloquence, speech, and acute intelligence, ever pursuing the path of the highest virtue, amiable to all, compassionate towards the poor, resisting the proud, and zealous for the promotion of others. He was liberal and witty, ever on guard against deceiving or being deceived, at once the prudent child of this world and destined to become a child of light." Benedict, Prior of Canterbury and later Abbot of Peterborough, gives a similar assessment in the annals he contributed to the 'Thomas Saga' and did much to generate his posthumous fame and popularity.

Appointed Archdeacon

1153 was a momentous year. Blessed Eugenius III died in July and was succeeded by Anastasius IV. In September, Roger de Port l'Eveque had resigned as Archdeacon of Canterbury upon his appointment to the see of York. Thomas was chosen to succeed him and so became the most important and powerful dignitary in the English Church after bishops and abbots. Archbishop Theobald had already paved the way for Henry Plantegenet's arrival in England, and Stephen accepted him as king-in-waiting on condition that he himself could retain the crown for the remainder of his life. As it happened, Henry did not have to wait long because Stephen died at Dover Priory on 25th October that same year. Henry II was "unanimously elected king and anointed" by Theobald. Very soon the election of an English Pope, Hadrian IV, would add to a sense of golden expectation for the Church and State.

Henry II

Though Henry was only twenty-one when he became King, his initial attitude was all that could have been desired as he started to restore some equilibrium to his kingdom. He lived and worked at a determined pace and immediately called to account those barons who had grasped every opportunity offered by the chaos of Stephen's reign to wage war with one another and oppress the poor. He personally supervised every detail of government, had a remarkable memory for faces and facts, was competent in French and Latin, enjoyed the company of scholars, and was a generous patron of learning. Given the questionable moral standards prevailing at court, he was reasonably faithful in the exercise of his religious duties. However, he was prone to irrational bursts of rage, rarely sat down except at table or on horseback, constantly paced up and down, even during

Mass, had little consideration for others and, when he wished to move court, regularly ordered the royal retinue to pack up and move in the middle of the night.

Appointed Chancellor

Those who had held office under Stephen were willing to help the new king, but Henry preferred to rely on men nearer his own age, and this gave Archbishop Theobald the idea to introduce him to Thomas Becket, believing that the Church would be in safe hands if he became his Chancellor. Not only was Henry impressed but he remembered with gratitude the part Becket had played in securing his succession, and appointed him Chancellor in 1155. In those days the post-holder was not an official of the first rank, and gave precedence to the Justiciar and the Treasurer but, as one of the greatest men in the realm, Becket excelled as a model civil servant, and his skilful involvement in writs, charters, and the royal secretarial work, quickly led to the forging of a close and trusted friendship with Henry.

King and Chancellor were close enough in age to manage without formality, though Henry respected Becket's slight seniority, appreciated his experience, valued his calm temperament that balanced the royal volatility, and was grateful for the social graces he brought to the efficient arrangement of sumptuous entertainment. He never omitted anything that was appropriate to the royal honour, distributed charity effectively, was generous to the poor, won the admiration of the people, and attracted friendship for King and kingdom. When he was entrusted with embassies, he conducted himself with great versatility and style, not least when he negotiated the future marriage of the young Prince Henry to the French Princess Margaret, daughter of Louis VII. As eloquent in French as in English, on that occasion he impressed the French court by the splendour of his entourage and the generosity of the gifts he brought. Later when Henry and Louis argued over the succession to the county of Toulouse, he led four hundred knights in a military expedition on the King's behalf, personally fighting with skill and courage, and then arranged a treaty to the satisfaction of all parties. He helped Henry in restoring order to the kingdom, laid the foundations for future effective administration, reorganized the royal household, and rationalised the methods of collecting "scutage", those "shield payments" made by knights in lieu of military service. Everything pointed to a brilliant future in the political sphere for an outstanding royal official.

Trappings of power

Chancellor Becket was brilliant, rich, second only to the King and, on his own admission, "a proud, vain man, a feeder of birds…,of old the favourer of actors and follower of hounds". Some commentators say that his duties as Chancellor weighed heavily on his shoulders but, generally speaking, they are those who remembered him only as the saintly archbishop of later years, and could not imagine him enjoying the trappings of worldly power and pleasure that he undoubtedly did. They did not see that when he was immersed in public affairs and the secular grandeur of state, he could be proud, forceful, quick-tempered, and impetuous, and remained so all his life. In fact, Theobald, many of the clergy, and even John of Salisbury were disappointed that he did not use his office more energetically for the benefit of the Church. They felt he had ignored their interests and resented his appropriation of Church funds when the King needed a convenient source of revenue.

There was more tension between Church and State when, at Chichester in 1157, the Abbot of Battle Abbey refused to subject himself to the authority of the Bishop of Chichester on the grounds that William the Conqueror had granted the Abbey the privilege of autonomy. The Bishop claimed "that it was not lawful for any person, not even a king, to bestow ecclesiastical dignities, or grant ecclesiastical privileges to churches." In the event, the Abbot won his case, and one of those who voted against the Bishop was Chancellor Thomas Becket. As he lay dying in the early months of 1161, Archbishop Theobald came to the conclusion that he had made a mistake in proposing him as Chancellor, and wrote several times asking him to visit before it was too late, but Becket was in Normandy with the King and too busy to respond. Maybe it was embarrassment, distance, pressure of State business, or an unwillingness to be involved in inevitable discussion about the succession to Canterbury that kept him away. Theobald descrved a visit from Becket and Henry, and it is sad that he died on 11th April, without that small comfort.

The King and the Archbishop

People do not become saints overnight just as the embryo does not fully reflect mature development, but there were signs that Becket was no ordinary mortal and much more than a politician. He welcomed into his house all those who wanted to enhance their culture and lead a virtuous life, and the young nobility including Prince Henry who came to learn from his scholarship and experience, were conscious of the sense of holiness that he radiated. In a licentious court, no breath of scandal ever touched him and his confessor testified to his blameless life in the face of extreme temptation. When moral issues were at stake, he was always ready to brave the King's fearsome anger, and protested vigorously when he took Stephen's daughter Mary out of her convent and married her off to a son of the Count of Flanders. He prayed long hours into the night, used the discipline, had frequent recourse to the Sacrament of Penance, spent Holy Week in retreat at Merton Priory, and took it to heart when Aschetinus, the Prior of Leicester Abbey, rebuked him for spending so much time playing chess, and his vain choice of fashionable clothes. Most significantly perhaps, he inspired great love in twelfth century people who were well able to recognise examples of true Christian virtue.

Appointed Archbishop

King and Chancellor were still in Normandy when Theobald died and the see of Canterbury fell vacant. It stayed that way for a year, a fortunate circumstance for the royal treasury that, according to custom, received all revenues until the appointment was made. In 1162, Henry ordered that arrangements be made to ensure his son's eventual and smooth succession by having him crowned co-regent, and demanded that the fealty of prelates and barons should be secured before any ceremony took place. There were signs of restlessness in Wales and he asked Becket to go and calm things down. As the Chancellor took his leave at Falaise Castle, Henry said, "You do not yet fully comprehend the reason for your mission. It is my intention that you should become Archbishop of Canterbury." Becket glanced down at his splendid attire and answered with some irony, "How religious, how saintly is the man you would appoint to that holy see," and prophesied, "the love that is now so great between us would be changed to the most bitter hatred. I know that you would make many demands which I could never bear with equanimity."

Premonitions

Nevertheless, a commission formed by the bishops of Chichester, Exeter and Rochester, the Abbott of Battle, and the Justiciar Richard de Lacy went to Canterbury to convene the chapter. Wilbert, the Cathedral Prior met with senior monks who had early reservations about accepting an Archbishop who was not a member of a monastic order, but they decided that Becket's virtues outweighed their misgivings. The English bishops and abbots held a meeting and, with the exception of Gilbert Foliot of Hereford, approved his appointment. He was still reluctant because he was certain that the King's ecclesiastical policy would clash with his duty to the Church, but the Papal Legate, Cardinal Enrico Moricotti of Pisa, eventually persuaded him that it was what God wanted for the Church in England. Bishop Walter of Rochester ordained him to the priesthood on Ember Saturday, 12th June 1162, and Bishop Henry de Blois of Winchester consecrated him Archbishop the following day, the first Sunday after Pentecost. This is now the Solemnity of the Most Holy Trinity that the new Archbishop was the first to introduce before its extension to the universal Church by Pope John XXII in 1334.

Since the King was in France, it was Prince Henry who announced the royal approval before the assembled bishops, monks, nuns, and clergy. Huge crowds of the laity acclaimed their new Archbishop with enthusiasm, but he took no notice of the adulation as he "advanced on foot with great humility and contrition, the tears flowing from his eyes as he thought less of the honour given to him than the burden imposed." On 10th August, the feast of St

Lawrence, Deacon and Martyr, he received from the high altar of the Cathedral the pallium that had been sent by Pope Alexander III who had succeeded Hadrian IV in 1159.

Seeds of conflict

Henry had taken it for granted that the new Archbishop would continue to serve him as Chancellor and help him implement his plans for limiting the power of the Church. He did not realise that his friend was more than a courtier and had his own determined principles. Henry was well aware of his strength of character, logical mind, and wholehearted commitment to responsibility, but had not guessed that these would now be brought to the service of God with episcopal dignity and fearless devotion to the rights of the Church. Thomas' initial fears were soon to be realised for, within a year, he would find it necessary to oppose Henry on a matter of State administration, and cause royal irritation by his determination to recover Canterbury's alienated property including that which had fortuitously come into the possession of the Crown.

As Chancellor, Thomas had managed to keep his profound spirituality more or less unobserved, but once he was Archbishop it could no longer be concealed. People thought there had been an immediate transformation in habits and character because they did not know that the seeds of sanctity had already been sown in receptive soil. In mediaeval times, bishops whose cathedrals were staffed by monks were technically abbots, and the new Archbishop was immediately sensitive to the feelings of the Prior and Canterbury community of Christ Church who had been deprived by royal pressure of their privilege of electing their Archbishop. He gave them great comfort and confidence by going to Merton to be clothed in the habit of the Canons Regular of Saint Augustine.

Holiness of life

He was punctilious in the productive observance of the monastic Rule, rose at dawn to say Mass, and afterwards meditated and studied in the cloister of the Cathedral priory. He dined with the community and guests about three o'clock in the afternoon and, though he denied himself, kept a good table for the sake of others. He considered one of his most important episcopal duties was to select candidates for holy orders with the greatest care, because the health of the Church, the administration of the Sacraments, the celebration of the sacrifice of the Mass, evangelisation, and the salvation of souls was dependent on the quality of the ministerial priesthood. William FitzStephen tells us that beneath his monastic habit he "wore a knee-length hair shirt from which he did not try to remove the little insects that made their home there, and regularly took the discipline; he ate little and drank only water in which hay had been boiled; he listened to scripture readings during meals and discussed theology with scholars after supper. He doubled the almsgiving of his predecessor and, at ten o'clock every morning, welcomed beggars to his house, washed their feet, and fed them."

Gregorian Reform

Religious revival in Europe and the monastic reform exemplified by Cluny, marked the beginning of a period of Church renewal that was given impetus and direction by Pope St Leo IX, 1049-1054, whose process of eradicating abuses in the Church started with the papacy itself. He regularized election procedures, defined the role of cardinals, appointed reformers to key positions in the Church, and summoned provincial councils to implement decisions. Pope Nicholas II continued in like manner, but it was the pontificate of Pope St Gregory VII, 1073-1085, that determined the course of ecclesiastical reform for the next fifty years and gave it its name. At the heart of the reform agenda was the liberation of the Church from the compromising secular entanglements of lay investiture, the buying and selling of clerical appointments known as simony, and clerical marriage. Celibacy was promoted as a worthy aim for all consecrated to the service of God, and a prevention of the potentially scandalous bequests of church property to clerical offspring.

Lay Investiture

In the early Middle Ages, secular rulers often chose candidates for vacant bishoprics. During the consecration, the bishop-elect paid homage to the ruler who invested him with the lands attached to the see, and presented him with the episcopal crozier and ring, a sign that he expected his loyalty and obedience. The Church saw the dangers of unwarranted secular intrusion into ecclesiastical affairs, and in 1075, St Gregory issued a decree forbidding such investitures. This led to problems with the German emperor Henry IV that continued for fifty years before Pope Callistus II and the emperor Henry V reached a compromise. At the Diet (Council) of Worms in 1122, the emperor relinquished the rights to appoint bishops and invest them with ring and crozier, but retained reception of the bishop's homage in exchange for the diocesan lands

In England, Henry II wanted to limit the Church autonomy that had grown during Stephen's anarchic reign, and that clashed with his views on royal autocracy. The Church's position had been further strengthened by the implementation of reform, the development of Canon Law, the increased independence of church courts from secular jurisdiction, and the latitude of taking appeals to Rome. Henry was convinced that his Norman ancestors like William the Conqueror would never have tolerated such ecclesiastical independence, and expected Becket to help him re-establish what he considered to be his rights over the Church in England. Thomas was well aware that this is what Henry had in mind when he nominated him to the see of Canterbury and had warned him that the co-operation he expected could not be forthcoming. At this stage, however, the King was still confident that he could persuade his friend to change his mind.

The Archbishop and Prince Henry went to Southampton to greet Henry upon his return to England. He was annoyed that Thomas had resigned as Chancellor because this looked like a determination to break with the past, but they were still friends as they rode back together to London. On the way, Thomas outlined the difficulties of recovering the land-holdings and rents of Canterbury that had been seized by previous rulers and barons during periods when the see was vacant. Henry approved his recovery plan, but it struck home that the relationship he wanted when he arranged the Archbishop's election was not to be. Back in London trouble was soon brewing and FitzStephen records that, as soon as Thomas became identified with the cause of ecclesiastical liberty, "the King's courtiers seeking to win his favour and itching to gain his ear, defamed the Archbishop and hated him without cause."

Crisis in Rome

When Pope Alexander had been elected in 1159, two dissident votes had been cast for Cardinal Octavian who had reacted by dragging the papal vestments from him and declaring himself anti-pope Victor IV. Circumstances in Rome became so fraught that Alexander had to withdraw to Nympha, south east of the capital, for his coronation and things were made worse when the Holy Roman Emperor, Frederick I Barbarosa, declared his allegiance to Victor. Henry, however, supported Alexander and this gave him the leverage to propose the canonisation in 1161 of Edward the Confessor, King from 1042 to 1066, who was a blood relative through his great-grandmother, St Margaret of Scotland.

At Easter in 1163, Alexander summoned a council in Tours. Henry allowed the Archbishops of Canterbury and York to attend provided this did not compromise royal authority, nor create an opportunity to introduce new regulations in England.

Given the delicacy of his situation in a schism that was to last eighteen years, Alexander did not want to lose Henry's good will by granting too many favours to the Church in England. However, the extraordinary welcome Thomas received in France, where he was given precedence over the seventeen cardinals, one hundred and twenty bishops, and four hundred and fourteen abbots who attended, helped him win from Alexander a guarantee of Canterbury's privileges. He presented the Pope with his biography to date written by John of Salisbury, and requested the canonization of his great predecessor Anselm.

While Thomas was away, his enemy Gilbert Foliot was translated from the See of Hereford to London where he was enthroned in St Paul's on 28th April 1163. Thomas sent him a friendly letter welcoming him as his senior suffragan, but Foliot refused to pay homage to his Archbishop on the grounds that he had already performed this duty to Theobald when appointed to Hereford in 1147. On 13th October, the relics of the newly canonized Edward the Confessor were solemnly translated to a new shrine in Westminster Abbey. Henry and Thomas both attended, but it would be the last time they would meet as friends. In the feudal world every vassal swore fealty to his liege lord, and people owed homage to a king as ruler of the land and to God as supreme ruler. For the majority these two loyalties can run parallel but for Thomas Becket they were to clash.

Early disputes

The division between King and Archbishop had a relatively trivial beginning. One of the King's tenants, William of Eynsford in Kent, had attacked a priest who had been appointed to the parish there, and Thomas had felt it necessary to excommunicate him. Henry saw this as a slight on his own authority and his fury erupted so, in a spirit of reconciliation, Thomas absolved the culprit. Then Philip de Brois, a canon of Bedford, who had been found innocent in the Bishop of Lincoln's court of murdering a knight, refused to face a retrial in the sheriff's court. Thomas took him under his protection and, in the Archbishop's court, with Henry's ambassadors present, the canon admitted that he had been rude to the sheriff and was sentenced to stand naked before him to apologise, and promise to live in subjection to him in the future. This did not satisfy Henry who wanted him hanged for insulting royal authority.

Intrusion of secular power

William the Conqueror had established ecclesiastical courts in order to withdraw clerics from civil courts. In the light of the de Brois case, Henry found this apparent curtailment of royal power intolerable and was aggrieved at the thought that the crimes of clerics might go unpunished or be treated leniently. He made a number of attempts through his justiciars to assert his right to judge members of the clergy accused of crime and, at the Council of Westminster in 1163, demanded that "clerks seized or convicted of serious crimes should be deprived of the protection of the Church and handed over to his officers" to be tried in the secular courts. Thomas opposed the finding on the grounds that it transgressed Canon Law, and such a process would involve two trials and two sentences for the same offence. He pointed out that "not even God judges the same matter twice." The King resorted to "the ancient custom of the realm", and referred to pre-Conquest times when spiritual and secular cases were tried together by bishop and ealdorman in the one shire-court.

Thomas did not intend that clergy who had broken the law should escape justice, but he regarded it as his duty to make sure that they were not deprived of a century old privilege. If that were to happen, the Church would once again be dominated by the secular power that Popes and Bishops had tried to keep at bay. Like other Church leaders in the twelfth century he was versed in the philosophy governing Church-State relations and felt obliged to resist the intrusion of secular power, mainly because justice systems had not yet been centralized, and it was only fair that the clergy should have the same rights that were enjoyed by many other professions, guilds and trades.

Royal confiscation and anger

Thomas pleaded with Henry not to ignore the customs and practice of Christendom but the King was not to be moved. All the bishops then met in consultation and, almost to a man, reminded Henry that they had "sworn fealty to him in life and limb and earthly honour, 'saving their order' (except when spiritual responsibilities otherwise required), that in the term 'earthly honour' was comprehended the royal customs, and that they would by no means bind themselves in another form." An enraged Henry told them that "poison lurked in the phrase 'saving their order'", and immediately declared that all castles and honours that Thomas had received in his capacity as Chancellor were confiscate to the Crown.

The King called a meeting at Northampton and, according to Roger de Pontigny, sent Thomas a message saying that accommodation had not yet been arranged for him, and he had to wait patiently at the roadside until it was ready. He was then berated again for earlier opposition and reminded that he owed everything to the royal friendship. He replied that he was not ungrateful and said he would never oppose the King's will when it coincided with the will of God. "I don't want a sermon from you"; you are just the son of one of my villeins," retorted Henry. Thomas replied, "I am ready for your honour and good pleasure, saving my order; but on those things which concern your honour and the salvation of your soul, you should have consulted me who you have found faithful and useful in counsel, rather than those who have kindled a flame of envy and strive to take vengeance on me who have done them no harm." The two parted without any meeting of minds.

Henry asserts royal jurisdiction

In the matter of the Church's right to deal with criminal clerics, the Archbishop's position was suddenly undermined by his brother bishops Roger of York, Gilbert of London and Hilary of Chichester who announced their support of the King. Many other bishops, some cardinals, and even Pope Alexander recommended submission, and reluctantly he gave way. Henry thought he now had Thomas on the run, and tried to exploit his advantage by calling the bishops and barons to a council at Clarendon, one of his favourite hunting lodges near Salisbury. Without any preamble or discussion, he presented them with his conclusions that were to be known as the Constitutions of Clarendon. The Queen Mother Matilda was convinced her son had made an error of judgement and that the codification failed to take into consideration the tenth century developments in Church-State relations. She was thinking of what had already been described as Gregorian Reform and Lay Investiture.

Henry ignored his mother's concern and ordered that in future:

- disputes about the bestowal of benefices must be put before royal courts;

- no church was to be erected on royal land without royal permission;

- according to the offence, criminal clerks must be tried in a royal court or in a church court but, in this latter case, the King could review the case tried and the Church must not protect the accused;

- bishops and clergy must not leave England without royal permission;

- if a bishop or archdeacon makes an accusation against a person living on royal land and he refuses satisfaction, he may not be excommunicated before being summoned to make amends before the King's officer (a clear infringement of spiritual jurisdiction);

- archbishops, bishops and other crown tenants hold their lands subject to feudal custom;

- the Church may not hold property forfeited to the Crown even if it is on land owned by the Church;

- the King must receive the revenues of sees, abbeys and priories that are vacant pending appointment;

- elections must be held in the royal chapel, wherever it is at the time, receive the King's assent, and the elect must do homage before taking office;

- sons of villeins may not be ordained to the priesthood without the consent of the liege-lord.

On the advice of bishops and barons, Thomas was conciliatory at first and accepted the document so that he could have the precise details in writing before deliberating on the implications. On the way from Clarendon to Winchester, he talked to his domestic clerics about the events of the Council. Some said he had acted prudently on the grounds of expediency, but his forthright cross-bearer, Alexander Llewelyn, told him he had betrayed the Church. With awful realisation, Thomas groaned, "I repent and am aghast at my transgression, and judge myself henceforth unworthy as a priest to approach Him whose Church I have so basely sold. I will sit silent in grief until the 'day-spring' from on high hath visited me' (*Lk* 1:78) and until I am worthy to be absolved by God and the lord Pope." As soon as the return journey was over, he suspended himself from saying Mass and did severe penance in sackcloth and ashes. He made an unsuccessful attempt to leave the country, and it is noticeable that he did not ask for Henry's permission as the Clarendon Constitutions stipulated.

Henry inflicts penalties on Becket

In time, as a growing number of bishops capitulated to the royal position, Henry began to hope that Thomas would resign. To apply pressure, he summoned him to another council at Northampton Castle to answer several charges levelled against him. On 8th October, 1164, he was accused of treasonable contempt for the Crown because he had not dealt personally with the application made by the Exchequer clerk, John the Marshall, for a piece of land near Chichester. Without any defence being allowed, the Bishop of Winchester was ordered to read the sentence that he must forfeit all his goods and throw himself upon the King's mercy. Though the other bishops advised Thomas to submit to the judgement, they at least had the decency to stand surety for him except, of course, Gilbert Foliot of London.

Later that same day, Thomas was forced to pay back £300 that he had spent making necessary repairs in fulfilling his responsibility as Guardian of the castles of Eye and Berkhamstead, and refurbishing the Tower of London. On 9th October he was ordered to surrender all the revenues of Canterbury that had accrued while the see was vacant, and the income from all the other sees and abbeys that been temporarily vacant during his time as Chancellor. He consulted with the other bishops and they recommended a payment of two thousand marks, but Henry rejected the offer. A few colleagues urged him to stand his ground but others like the timorous Hilary of Chichester thought he should throw himself upon the King's mercy. On 12th October, the strain had taken its toll and it is not surprising that he was unwell, but Henry thought he was malingering and sent messengers demanding security for the revenues from the vacant sees and abbeys. Thomas said he would reply in person the next day if he had recovered.

Becket before Henry's court

He celebrated Mass at daybreak the following morning and was consoled by the words of the Introit, "Though princes sit plotting against me, I ponder on your statutes. Your will is my delight; your statutes my counsellors" (*Ps* 118:23). He returned to the Council still in his vestments, Alexander Llewelyn leading the way with his cross. When the bishops were assembled, his friend Herbert of Bosham muttered to him that he had every right to excommunicate anyone who laid hands on him, but William FitzStephen more gently advised, "pray for them and forgive them." To be fair, most of the bishops tried to intercede for their Archbishop and explained that the Church of Canterbury would face ruin if all his goods were confiscated. When they added that Thomas had called them to answer to a papal court for their share in any judgement made against him, Henry threw another tantrum. He insisted that the Archbishop was his liege-man with no right of appeal, asserted inaccurately that he had sworn obedience to royal courts at Clarendon, and demanded an account of his time as Chancellor. Thomas delivered a calm and measured statement, concluding "I still appeal, and I place both my person and the Church of Canterbury under the protection of God and the Pope." Some were impressed, others were concerned about what previous kings had done to disobedient churchmen but, in general, the bishops refused to join in the condemnation of the Archbishop.

Open dispute

Henry now commanded the barons, the lords temporal to pass judgement, and the Earl of Leicester spoke for them: "The King commands you to render your accounts. Otherwise you must hear judgement." "Judgement?" queried Thomas. "I was given the church of Canterbury free from temporal obligations. Son and earl listen: you are bound to obey God and me before your earthly king. Neither law nor reason allows children to judge their father and condemn him. Wherefore I refuse the king's judgement and yours, and everybody's under God. I will be judged only by the Pope. You, my fellow bishops, who have served man rather than God, I summon to the presence of the Pope. And so, guarded by the authority of the Catholic Church and the Holy See, I go from here."

To the cries of "Traitor!" Thomas walked to the door which, according to FitzStephen opened of its own accord despite having been barred. Herbert of Bosham felt that "If I were to be silent about such a sentence, future ages will not do so, for this is a new form of judgement, perhaps in accordance with the new rules promulgated at Clarendon. Such a thing has never been known, that an Archbishop of Canterbury should be tried in the court of a king. It is contrary to the dignity of the Church and the authority of his person."

Escape to France

Once outside and mounted, Thomas was greeted with such enthusiasm by crowds of people asking him to bless them that he had a problem controlling his horse. With the knights who served in his retinue and a few of his brother bishops, he went to the Cluniac monastery of St Andrew where he talked with friends and "was happy because he had been deemed worthy to suffer for the name of Jesus". After supper, and when his loyal knights had renewed their fealty and departed, he sent Walter of Rochester, Robert of Hereford and Roger of Worcester to ask the King for safe-conduct and his permission to depart, but Henry maliciously delayed his reply. Even though the town crier had gone around announcing that the Archbishop must not be harmed, Thomas still suspected violence and thought it best to leave Northampton that night so that the position of the Church should not be made more invidious because of his conflict with the King. He went to Eastry Palace in Kent where he lodged for eight days and then, on 2nd November, left Sandwich for France in a fishing boat with a few faithful friends.

Exile and Martyrdom

Henry's next ploy was to send a group of bishops and barons to Pope Alexander at Sens with a list of accusations against Thomas. The Pope called a consistory but did not allow any representations to be made until Herbert of Bosham arrived to speak on behalf of the Archbishop. Gilbert Foliot, inimical as ever, demanded that there should be no appeal but the Pope quashed him with, "That is my privilege which I will not give to another; when he is to be judged he will be judged by us, for it were against all reason to send him back to England to be judged by his adversaries."

By now, Thomas was in Flanders where he had made straight for the Cistercian Abbey of St Bertin at St Omer. As a matter of courtesy, he sent deputies to King Louis VII of France to say that he had arrived. The message was received graciously and returned with a warm promise of protection in French dominions, which was just as well since Henry had written to Louis describing Thomas as the "former archbishop." Louis commented that "like the King of England, I am also a king, but I have no power over the least of my clerks of my realm." Greatly moved by what Thomas' friends had to say he added, "Henry, before he dealt so harshly with one who had been so great a friend and so great an archbishop should have remembered the verse, 'Be angry and sin not' (*Ep* 4:26)", and emphasised his promise of protection for the exile throughout his dominions.

Wish to resign as Archbishop

Thomas decided the time had come to make a personal visit to the Pope, and went to Sens on 29th November 1164 to show him the Clarendon Constitutions. With a slightly unfair wisdom of hindsight, Alexander said he should not have given them even the slightest consideration. At that point, Thomas admitted that his election may not have been in accordance with canon Law and he had not acquitted himself well in his office, though he had accepted the Archbishopric with reluctance after persuasion by the Papal Legate. He thereupon resigned his see of Canterbury and delivered his episcopal ring to the Pope. Some cardinals thought that this was a convenient solution but the majority hailed him as a champion of the Church and insisted that he should be reinstated. Alexander did so immediately with a reminder that he could not abandon God's cause, and recommended a visit to the Cistercian Abbey of Pontigny.

Thomas appreciated the monastery as an ideal retreat, a school of expiation for sins, and would not allow any favours or special treatment. He devoted himself to prayer and fasting, was clothed in the Benedictine habit, and wrote many letters to supporters and opponents alike, though these brought no lasting resolution of problems. His inclusion in the Benedictine calendar of its saints' feasts indicates that he renewed his monastic vows about this time. Meanwhile, Henry confiscated the property of the Archbishop's friends, domestics and supporters, and ordered them to visit him so that he might be moved by the distressing situation into which he had put them. Many did come to Potigny but only to offer their continued support, while Henry threatened the Abbot that he was about to seize Cistercian properties in his realm. When the Abbot hinted to Thomas that it might be better if he left, he went to St Columba's Abbey near Sens as the guest of King Louis.

Pope annuls King's sentence

In June 1165, Pope Alexander annulled the sentence passed on Thomas at Northampton, but advised him not to take any action against Henry before Easter 1166. The King had already said that he had a mind to force English bishops to transfer their allegiance to the new anti-pope Pascal III whose election in 1164 had again been supported by Barbarosa. Bishops John of Oxford and Richard of Ilchester, who had tried to persuade Alexander to approve the Clarendon Constitutions, attended as their King's representatives and had sworn allegiance to Pascal in his name. That Henry later retracted the oath did little to alleviate Alexander's precarious position.

Persecutions and excommunications

Thomas had written three times to Henry alerting him to the possible consequences of persecuting the Church of Canterbury. Alexander's prohibition of taking measures against the King expired at Easter 1166 and, at Vezelay on Whitsunday 12th June, Thomas excommunicated John of Oxford, Richard of Ilchester, Jocelyn of Salisbury who had collaborated in drawing up the Clarendon constitutions, Hugh first Earl of Norfolk and "all who might conspire against the see of Canterbury and its occupant in the future." By October 1169, twenty more names had appeared on the excommunication list, including that of Gilbert Foliot of London, and others who were intent on despoiling the Church of Canterbury. Many English bishops thought it was time for the Pope to be involved and, in answer to their appeal, Alexander appointed Cardinals William of Pavia and Otto of Ostia as his legates to try and resolve the impasse. The plan was doomed to failure.

Reconcilliation attempted

On 18th November 1169, the kings of England and France met with Thomas, the Archbishop of Rouen, and the Papal Legate Vivian at Montmartre. Henry was worried that Thomas might place England under interdict, the sentence which the Church passes and prohibits a person or an entire population from taking part in public worship and receiving the sacraments, and he was now prepared to rescind the

Clarendon Constitutions. For his part, Thomas was willing to return to England but, on the Pope's advice, this was conditional on Henry giving him the kiss of peace, not the liturgical symbol but a civil ceremony that marked the conclusion of agreements with a guarantee of good faith and a pledge of security. Unfortunately, Henry declined on the specious grounds that in one of his rages he had sworn an oath never to kiss Thomas again. Thomas insisted in vain and the meeting ended with nothing accomplished.

Flawed coronation

In March 1170, Henry made a monumental mistake. During a king's lifetime, it was feudal practice to crown the eldest son to ensure peaceful succession to the throne, but he arranged for the coronation of Prince Henry as co-regent without consulting the Archbishop of Canterbury whose prerogative it was to conduct the solemn ceremony, or delegate it to his senior suffragan. Letters from Pope Alexander and Becket forbidding this were ignored and, in a move of calculated defiance, Roger of York crowned the Prince with the assistance of Gilbert Foliot of London, Jocelyn of Salisbury, Walter of Rochester, and Hugh of Durham. It was a measure of the nation's respect for Thomas that there was widespread disapproval and, after issuing a sharp rebuke, the Pope empowered Thomas to suspend Roger of York and excommunicate the collaborators.

Ten days later, Henry went to France after receiving a letter from the Pope warning him that Thomas was entitled to impose an interdict on his continental realm. To add to his woes, he found Louis VII angry that his daughter Margaret, Prince Henry's wife, had not been included in her husband's coronation. On the Pope's instructions, he eventually met Thomas on 22nd July, 1170, at a place called the Traitor's Field at Freteval near Maine. The question of the kiss of peace was avoided but Thomas asked permission to apply the sanctions authorised by the Pope to his suffragans for their part in the coronation. Henry agreed, Thomas dismounted and knelt before him, and the King said their friendship was resumed, but his sincerity is in some doubt because shortly afterwards he told Arnulf, the compliant bishop of Lisieux to tell Thomas that he wanted all who had been excommunicated to be absolved, but the Archbishop refused because they had not yet made reparation. Henry then issued a writ to Prince Henry concerning the restoration of diocesan property stating, with some exaggeration "that Thomas, Archbishop of Canterbury, has made peace with me according to my will".

Return to England

On 24th November 1170, Thomas was at Wissant, not far from Calais, on his way back to England, and there, he renewed the excommunication of Roger of York and the bishops who had taken part in the irregular coronation.

Two days later, he landed at Sandwich to a rapturous reception by the people of Canterbury who came to meet him, as did the parishioners of churches along the route who formed welcoming processions. Herbert of Bosham wrote that "Christ's poor received him with victor's laurels and, as the Lord's anointed, wherever he went people, great and small, young and old, flocked to meet him, strewing their garments in front of him and crying, 'Blessed is he who comes in the name of the Lord.'"

On 1st December, the Cathedral resounded to his arrival with pealing bells, organ voluntaries, a fanfare of trumpets, and at Mass the restored Archbishop preached on the text, "For there is no eternal city for us in this life but we look for one in the life to come" (*Heb* 13:14). When he had exchanged the kiss of peace with his attending clergy, a prescient Herbert of Bosham went to him and said, "My lord, it matters not to us now when you depart out of this world, since today in you Christ's spouse, the Church, has conquered, nay rather, Christ Himself conquers, Christ reigns, Christ rules." In the years to come Canterbury would celebrate 1st December as the feast of the Return of St Thomas.

Thomas 'this turbulent priest'

Early in December, Roger of York, Gilbert of London and Jocelyn of Salisbury complained to the King about their excommunication and fabricated an elaborate accusation against Thomas. They concocted the story that he was going about at the head of an army and, in what amounted to an invitation to murder, warned Henry would have no peace while Thomas lived. Henry's fury was immediately ignited. "I have nourished and promoted in my realm idle and wretched knaves, faithless to their lord who they allow to be mocked so shamefully by a low-born clerk." He rebuked all who had allowed an impudent cleric to live and disturb him, but there is no unanimity that he asked, "Who will rid me of this turbulent priest?" Nevertheless, the implication that Becket had lived long enough brought an immediate reaction from four knights of his court: Reginald Fitzurse, one of Becket's own tenants, William de Tracy who had been his liege-man during his Chancellorship, Hugh de Morville, and Richard the Breton. They thought they had heard enough and did not wait for the royal temper to cool. When Henry calmed down, he realised with horror what they might do and sent messengers to stop them. They came back with the news that they had already left France, so he thought the safest course was to issue a warrant for the Archbishop's arrest, but he was too late.

His life under threat

Thomas celebrated Midnight Mass of the Nativity in his Cathedral and chose as the text of his sermon, "On earth, peace to men of good will." He shared with his congregation the thought that Canterbury already had one martyred Archbishop (St Alphege, 1006-12, who had been killed by the Danes at Greenwich), and predicted that there would soon be another. On 26th December, the feast of the first Christian martyr St Stephen, he presided at High Mass. The following day, the feast of St John the Evangelist, a letter arrived warning him that southeast Kent was in a state of ominous expectation. He sent Herbert of Bosham and Alexander Llewelyn to France so that, should he be killed, they would be safe from Henry's further malevolence. He then instructed Gilbert de Glanville, bishop of Rochester, to take his report of events to the Pope, and absolved some priests who had continued to say Mass while under censure.

Announcing that they were acting in the name of the King, the four knights mustered an armed force made up of the retainers of Robert de Broc who held a grudge against the Archbishop because he had excommunicated him for deliberately injuring the horse of a poor man who was in the service of the diocese. They marched on Canterbury and arrived there about three o'clock in the afternoon of 29th December. Thomas was talking to a small group in the community house while others were still in the refectory. The knights burst in, boorishly ignored the courteous offer of refreshment, and demanded that the Archbishop be told that the King's messengers wanted to see him. Thomas came to greet them and asked the purpose of their visit, only to be answered with curses. When Fitzurse asked if he wanted them to speak to him in public or private, he said that these things should be spoken for all to hear.

Fitzurse began by upbraiding the Archbishop for taking offence over the matter of Prince Henry's coronation, and for showing ingratitude for the King's clemency by excommunicating the bishops of York. London and Salisbury. Thomas answered that he bore no animosity towards the Prince, and that it was the Pope himself who had ordered the excommunications. "It was through you," they bellowed; "do you absolve them?" Thomas replied that he had no authority to absolve what the Pope had condemned. "Well then," they retorted, "this is the King's command that you depart with all your men from the kingdom and lands of his dominion." Henry had given no such order.

"Leave your threats and your brawling," advised Thomas. "I put my trust in the King of Heaven for, from this day forth, no one shall ever see the sea between me and my Church. I have not come back to flee again; here shall he who wants me find me." When the knights rebuked him for failing to respect the King, he continued "Whoever shall presume to violate the decrees of the Holy Roman See or the laws of Christ's Church, and refuse to come of his own accord to make restitution, I will not spare him." "You have spoken in peril of your death," they warned. "Are you come to slay me?" he asked. "I am not moved by your threats, nor are your swords more ready to strike than is my soul for martyrdom." The four knights left to arm themselves as Thomas consoled his bewildered and frightened clergy.

Murder in the Cathedral

Five of the Archbishop's biographers - Edward Grim, William Fitzstephen, John of Salisbury, William of Canterbury, and Abbot Benedict of Peterborough witnessed what transpired. Herbert of Bosham and Roger of Pontigny were elsewhere but were able to provide well-informed accounts. Because of the rapid succession of events, details do not always harmonize, but there is general agreement. Edward Grim had only recently arrived in Canterbury, and his contribution to English Historical Documents II probably offers the most impartial narrative.

When the knights returned fully armed, they found the doors barred. They received no response to their loud knocks, so they went to the back of the house to the orchard and broke in through a wooden partition. The community was now thoroughly alarmed and some fled for safety while others begged Thomas to take refuge in the Cathedral. At first, he was reluctant and said, "Here shall he who wants me find me," and continued to wait even when they reminded him that it was time for

Vespers. Eventually he gave way and there was an orderly and dignified procession along the cloister to the Cathedral led by a monk carrying the Archbishop's cross.

Vespers were already being sung, but some of the community came to receive Thomas at the transept door that he asked them to leave unlocked. At this point, John of Salisbury and a number of others took refuge behind altars and in the Cathedral's dark recesses leaving only William FitzStephen, Edward Grim and Robert of Merton standing by their Archbishop. Robert had been prior of Merton during his schooldays there and was now his confessor. The knights charged through the transept with swords at the ready but they could not see much in the December gloom. Thomas was standing a little way up the steps that led to the north choir isle and was partly obscured by the pillar at the corner of the staircase. "Where is Thomas Becket, traitor to the King?" they yelled, but he had no intention of answering to such an inaccurate description. They thought better of it and called, "Where is the Archbishop?" Now he revealed himself, coming slowly down to face them. "Here I am, no traitor to the King but a priest. What do you seek of me? Behold, I am ready to suffer in his name who redeemed me by his blood. Far be it from me to flee from your swords, or depart from righteousness."

Thomas turned to his right between the altars of the Most Blessed Virgin and St Benedict. The knights surrounded him and demanded that he absolve all those he had excommunicated and restore them to communion. He patiently explained that he was not empowered to do this before they had atoned for their offences. "Then you shall die this instant", they replied. The Archbishop responded, "I, too, am ready to die for my Lord so that in my blood the Church may obtain peace and liberty; but in the name of Almighty God, I forbid you to harm any of my men whether clerical or lay."

Even these violent men hesitated to murder the Archbishop in his own Cathedral, and they tried to drag him outside. Thomas who was no weakling threw three of them off but Fitzurse managed to cling on for a moment until flung away with a peremptory "Touch me not Reginald, you owe me fealty and obedience; you are acting like a madman." A raging Fitzurse replied, "Neither faith nor obedience do I owe you against my fealty to my lord the King," and he brandished his sword over the Archbishop's head in an unmistakeable threat. Thomas commended his soul to God, Our Blessed Lady, St Denis, and St Alphege his martyred predecessor. Fitzurse brought the blade down on his head with great force and Grim, who had bravely thrown his arms around his master to ward off the blow, was also wounded. Then de Tracy struck Thomas again on the head. Still he did not fall, but wiped the blood from his face murmuring, "Into thy hands I commend my spirit." When a third blow brought him to his knees, he breathed, "For the Name of Jesus and the protection of His Church, I am ready to embrace death." Richard the Breton struck him again as he knelt, fatally cutting open the skull. Thomas was by then so near the ground that the sword broke against the paving stones, and afterwards the pieces were kept on the Altar of the Sword's Point that was erected on the spot where Thomas died.

Funeral

For a while the Archbishop's body lay where it had fallen. The knights had gone and the townsfolk, now no longer afraid, poured into the transept and were aghast at what they saw. They dipped their clothes in the martyr's blood before the monks gently lifted his body and carried it to the choir where they kept vigil throughout the night. They were conscious of Robert de Broc's threat that if Thomas were not buried quickly, he would tear his body to pieces, so they prepared to have the funeral the following day. They took their Archbishop to the crypt and removed the habit of the Black Canons that he wore over his other clothes, and then the Cistercian habit he had adopted during his exile at Pontigny. It is said that, though he was tall and slim, this amount of clothing made him look portly, but it protected him from the cold from which he suffered because of poor circulation.

No one had realised the full extent of his self-denial until beneath his undergarments they found a lice-infested hair shirt. Edward Grim observed, "any one would have thought that the martyrdom of the day was less grievous than that which these small enemies continually inflicted." The Canterbury custom of embalming was omitted and the monks contented themselves with carefully washing the body before burial in a new marble tomb in the crypt. There was no Requiem because there could be no Mass in the Cathedral that had been desecrated by the spilling of blood.

King Henry's contrition

When Henry heard the news on New Year's Day 1171, he was devastated. According to Arnulf of Lisieux, "he put on sackcloth and ashes, and shut himself in his room for three days refusing food and drink and allowing no one to comfort him. He called on Almighty God to witness that he had neither willed the impious deed nor known that it had been committed." It has to be remembered that this bishop had a reputation for ingratiating himself and wanted to show the King in the most favourable light. When news of the slaughter reached Pope Alexander, he was so saddened that could not bring himself to talk about it and refused to allow anyone from England to come near him. He instructed Guillaume aux Blanches Mains, Archbishop of Sens, later of Reims and a Cardinal, to place Henry's continental domains under interdict, and condemned the murderers and all who had helped them. Henry's name was not on the excommunication list but he was forbidden to enter a church before papal legates had assessed the sincerity of his contrition.

Affairs of state took the King to Ireland in October 1171 and he managed to avoid the legates until May 1172 when he met them at Avranches. At first he adopted his fiery stance but eventually, with hand on the Gospel, he confessed that though he had neither wanted nor ordered it, he had been the cause of the murder and would accept whatever penance the legates imposed. He was sentenced to make two hundred knights available for crusading duties for a year, hold himself in readiness for three years to fight the infidel in Spain, restore Canterbury's lands, and pardon all those he had punished for supporting the Archbishop. The Clarendon Constitutions were not mentioned and the question of criminal clerics not raised thanks to the manoeuvres of Bishop Arnulf who made sure Henry escaped as lightly as possible. Henry's final words to the legates were, "My lords legates, I am entirely in your hands; rest assured that I am prepared to obey your commands. I will go to Jerusalem or Rome or St James' (shrine at Compostella), or elsewhere you order me." He then received absolution in church.

Increased power of State over Church

In the event, the obligation to fight in Spain was commuted to founding three monasteries, and King and Pope later agreed that any cleric charged with a criminal offence should not be tried before a lay tribunal unless forest laws had been infringed. However, it transpired that every obstacle was put in the way of clergy trials in church courts, the accused being imprisoned and his goods confiscated until he proved clerical status before a lay court. Henry's supposed contrition and acquiescence made little difference because he managed to keep a tight hold on the election of bishops and abbots, often deliberately delaying appointments so that he could rake in the revenues attached to the vacant see or abbey. He made sure that only those who supported him were appointed and his message when the see of Winchester fell vacant is an example: "Henry, King of England, to his faithful monks of the church of Winchester, greeting. I order you to hold a free election but, nevertheless, I forbid you to elect anyone except Richard of Ilchester."

It comes as something of a surprise that, despite demanding his atonement, Henry's subjects thought no less of him, and it is to their credit that they could distinguish between office and holder. The king was God's anointed to represent Him in secular government and, in their eyes, Henry's need for penitence in no way diminished the glorious power of the Crown. Stories abound as to what lay in store for the knights who martyred the Archbishop. Some say De Morville became Chief Justice in Eyre, north of the Trent, and one of the principal judges in England before doing penance in the Holy Land; de Tracy confessed to the Pope, gave his manor of Docombe to Canterbury in expiation, and was later appointed Grand Judiciary of Normandy; Fitzurse went to Ireland where he founded the clan MacMahon of Wexford, did penance in the Holy Land and died at Jerusalem; and Richard the Breton withdrew to his Devon estates where he eventually died of old age.

As far as the Church is concerned there is little left to say about the remainder of Henry's reign. Archbishop Richard who was appointed Thomas' successor to the See of Canterbury in 1174, was a wise and prudent pastor. In 1175, he called a Provincial Synod at Westminster in which provisions were made for the faithful observance of celibacy. Clerics in minor orders who had married were no longer eligible to hold benefices; subdeacons, deacons and priests were ordered to separate from the ladies they called wives because, for them, Canon Law forbade marriage. In 1176, in response to a request from Henry, the Pope sent Cardinal Hugo as papal legate to England to resolve various matters of business but, in the ecclesiastical sphere, he was unable to settle the difference of opinion between Canterbury and York regarding precedence. Eventually the Clarendon Constitutions became a dead letter.

Devotion to Saint Thomas

As Chancellor and Archbishop, Thomas attracted extraordinary admiration and affection in England and throughout Europe. News of his murder came as a profound shock to the whole of Christendom, and he was immediately acclaimed as a martyr for the cause of Christ and the authoritative liberty of the Church. Canterbury Cathedral remained closed until Easter 1171, by which time preparations had already been made for the admission of pilgrims. Benedict of Peterborough comments that the Archbishop's "marble coffin was enclosed by a wall of great hewn stones, firmly cramped together with mortar, iron and lead, with two windows in either side, at which those who came might insert their heads to kiss the sarcophagus."

Miracles wrought through Thomas' intercession were soon reported. In Canterbury three men, two women and a young boy were cured of their illnesses, sight was restored to a blind man, a dumbstruck visitor from Oxford recovered his speech, a child was cured of a deformity, and over the next decade seven hundred miracles were reported to have taken place at his tomb. The evidence of his sanctity was beyond doubt and, even before his successor had been appointed, Pope Alexander canonized him at Segni on 21st February 1173. The Church in England at once adopted him as her Patron, and for the next three centuries looked upon him as her pride and glory and the champion of her liberties.

Henry's public penance

On 12th and 13th July 1174 Henry II did public penance at the tomb in the crypt and was given a phial of the martyr's blood. He left Canterbury elated with such peace of mind that he galloped back to London without stopping. Later, that same year, the Cathedral chancel was damaged by fire, and later necessary renovation between 1179 and 1184 gave the monks led by William the Englishman an opportunity to create an enhanced shrine of St Thomas. They dismantled the chapel of the Holy Trinity where he had said his first Mass, transferred its altar to St John's chapel in the southeast transept, and then erected a Chapel of St Thomas in its place. As his name came to be invoked throughout the wider Church, the story of his martyrdom was told in sculpture, stained glass, frescoes, and illuminated manuscripts in Europe and the Holy Land. In 1175, his enamelled portrait was on the cover of the Gospel in Capua Cathedral and in a mosaic in Monreale Cathedral in 1178. Reliquaries made of Limoges enamel are now in the British Museum and with the Society of Antiquaries in London.

In 1220, Cardinal and Archbishop Stephen Langton of Canterbury arranged to translate the relics to the Chapel of St Thomas. He spent the eve of 7th July in prayer with the community and, at dawn, broke the seal of the sarcophagus and opened the coffin. Monks renowned for their holy lives lifted the skeleton and placed it in a new wooden casket bound with iron bands and enclosed in a gold-plated reliquary. At 9.00am, Archbishop Stephen with all his suffragans and prelates escorted the remains to the shrine newly embellished in gold plate and jewels by Walter of Colchester who was then sacristan at St Albans, and Elias of Dereham, a canon pf Salisbury. Archbishop William of Reims was the principle celebrant at the High Mass that followed, attended by a huge congregation that included King Henry III and the papal legate Pandulph who would later become bishop of Norwich and a cardinal. For the next three hundred years, the pilgrimage to the shrine became one of the most important in Europe, its depiction in the Cathedral's stained-glass windows a rich source of medieval life, and the Pilgrims' Way to Canterbury from London or Winchester can still be traced. The wider Christian world enriched the Canterbury shrine of St Thomas with offerings until it became one of the great sights of the western world, rivalling in splendour that of St James in Compostella.

Legacy

In terms of popular appeal, Thomas was the greatest English saint of the Middle Ages. Eighty churches were dedicated to him and, from the time of his death until 1538, one had only to call out the name "Thomas" in any town or village to be answered by half the male population. The dramatic circumstances of his death and the splendid courage with which he faced armed violence appealed to an era when physical heroism compelled admiration, and he was identified with the cause for which he died, namely the preservation of ecclesiastical liberty. Pilgrims to Canterbury did not always discuss the finer points of church-state relationships, but beneath their innocent Faith and excited conversation there was an awareness of St Thomas' stand against the encroachment of the Crown in Church affairs.

The ritual of anointing a ruler who is God's representative on earth, and who has been entrusted with His authority was considered so important that there were many legends about the miraculous arrival of the necessary oil. For example, the sacred vessel of oil, the "Sainte-Ampoule" was brought by a dove to be kept in Reims cathedral for the anointing of French Kings prior to the Revolution. In England, it was believed that Our Lady, the Queen of Heaven, had herself brought to St Thomas Becket of Canterbury the oil that was to be used to anoint England's rulers.

The Church had promoted pilgrimages to the Holy land, Rome and Santiago de Compostela as a form of penance and contrition for sins, with indulgences attached to shorten the cleansing time in Purgatory. The spirit of exile imposed by the journey was a reminder that sin can place a soul in exile from Heaven, and some undertook extended pilgrimages to demonstrate their flight from the world and, like the hermits in the desert, left home, possessions and temporal concerns. Later spirituality developed the concept of an inner journey and Saints Bonaventure, Teresa of Avila, and John of the Cross encouraged interior descents and ascents within the inner self to find God, and interpreted life on earth as a pilgrimage to the heavenly Jerusalem

Canterbury tales

The Pilgrimage to the relics and tomb of Saint Thomas is immortalised in Geoffrey Chaucer's *Canterbury Tales* written more than two hundred years after his death. A literal translation of the opening lines to the general *Prologue* gives a joyful sense of the passing of winter, milder weather, and roads more passable, and there is an element of deserved holiday in the pious journey for those who toil hard to make a living in a rural society.

"When April with its sweet showers has pierced the drought of March to the root, and bathed every vein of earth in such liquid that gives life to the flower; when

Zephyr, the West Wind, with sweet breath has brought the tender shoots in every wood and heath to life; and the young sun has completed its half-course in the Ram (the first stage in its annual journey through the signs of the Zodiac); and little birds sing and sleep all night with their eyes open; then Nature plants in human hearts the desire to go on pilgrimage, and palmers (who have made the pilgrimage to Jerusalem and brought back a palm-leaf) to look for shrines in foreign lands; and especially from the ends of every English county, they go to Canterbury to find the holy, blessed Martyr who helps them when they are ill."

Destruction of Becket's shrine by Henry VIII

For Catholics in England and beyond, St Thomas Becket represented the Church's right to act according to her laws, especially when the law of the land threatened human rights and the law of God, and he epitomised the ceaseless struggle of rendering both to God and to Caesar. In September 1538, three years after he had martyred Saints John Fisher and Thomas More for refusing to acknowledge the authority he claimed to have over the Church, Henry VIII was still confronting Pope Paul III, intending to govern his realm "without interference from any foreign princes or potentates". He launched a campaign against the cult of saints with particular hatred of St Thomas because he had placed papal authority before that of a secular ruler. In November, he issued a royal proclamation that "there appeareth nothing in his (Thomas') life and exterior conversation whereby he should be called a saint, but rather esteemed to be called a rebel and a traitor. Therefore, his Grace strictly chargeth and commandeth that from henceforth the said Thomas Becket shall not be called a saint, but Bishop Becket, and that his images and pictures shall be put down and avoided out of all churches, chapels, and other places; and the days to be festival in his name shall not be observed and all mention of his name removed from liturgy and books."

Henry's oppression of the cult of St Thomas was politically motivated in that he was worried that what he stood for was still alive and capable of inspiring insurrection, but the suppression of saints who attracted pilgrimages was also profitable to the Crown. Most shrines to be demolished were embellished with silver and gold, Winchester supplying a great cross of emeralds and Chichester three caskets of jewels, but that of St Thomas at Canterbury yielded the greatest prize of all "with two great chests of jewels such as six or eight strong men could do no more than convey one of them," and twenty-four wagons were needed to take away assorted treasures and precious objects. Apart from its financial significance, the destruction of the Martyr's tomb was an act of defiance against the Roman Pontiff.

When Pope Paul threatened drastic action, Henry was unmoved and retorted that Becket was "a rebel who fled to the realm of France and to the Bishop of Rome to procure the abrogation of wholesome laws."

It is hoped that the monks of Christ Church managed to save the precious relics and secretly buried them but, considering Henry's animosity, the obliteration was probably as complete as possible. A memorial shrine in a dedicated chapel of Canterbury Cathedral remains and when Pope John Paul II visited England in 1982, he prayed here with Archbishop Robert Runcie of Canterbury.

Bibliography

Butler's Lives of the Saints, Ed. M. Walsh, Burns and Oates, 1981

A History of the medieval Church, M. Deanesley, Methuen, London, 1951

From Domesday Book to Magna Carta, A. Poole, Clarendon Press, Oxford, 1955

The Earlier Tudors, J. Mackie, Clarendon Press, Oxford, 1952

The Catholic Church in England, Cardinal Gasquet, CTS, London, 1935

Glimpses of Catholic England, T. Westbrook, Burns and Oates, 1930

Saints and Ourselves, Ed. P. Caraman SJ, Hollis and Carter, London, 1958

History of England, H. Belloc, Methuen, London, 1927

Encyclopaedia of Catholicism, Harper and Collins, New York, 1995

History of Christianity, O. Chadwick, Weidenfeld and Nicolson, London, 1995

Canterbury, L. Goulder, Guild of Our Lady of Ransom, 1962

English Historical Documents, Volume II

The Divine Office, Collins, London, 1974

The Medieval Foundation, A Bryant, Collins, London, 1966

Life in Medieval England, J. Langley, Batsford, London 1960

The Turbulent Priest, P. Compton, Staples Press, London 1950